RONI
TAKES ACTION!

A CALL TO ACTION FOR A YOUNG GIRL WHO IS OVERWEIGHT

Written By:
Roni Roth Beshears, EdD, RDN
Registered Dietitian Nutritionist

Illustrated by:
Rob Peters

First U.S. edition 2014 (Chubby Roni Takes Action)
Second U.S. edition 2016 (Roni Takes Action)
First Hardcover edition 2019 (Roni Takes Action)

ISBN-13: 978-0-578-57055-6

Illustrations were done in pen and ink and 6B pencil on bristol paper and digitally painted in Photoshop.

All matters regarding weight management and health require medical supervision. The author is not engaged in rendering professional advice or services to children and their families or caregivers. The ideas, procedures and suggestions contained in this book are not intended as substitutes for consulting with your medical-care provider. All matters regarding weight management and health require medical supervision. The author shall not be liable or responsible for any loss or damage allegedly arising from the information or suggestions in this book. The author does not assume any responsibility for errors or for changes that occur after publication. The author does not have any control over and does not assume responsibility for author or third-party websites or their content.

To contact Dr. Roni Roth Beshears and to schedule a book and program presentation, please email her at roni.nutritionassociates@gmail.com.

For Mom:
The wind beneath my wings

— RRB

Acknowledgements

My personal story about being overweight as a child led to my interest in foods and nutrition at an early age and proved to be my vocation and avocation over time. Thanks to my high school guidance counselor for advising me to apply to an institution of higher learning with a course of study in dietetics. The conception of this book occurred while taking a children's picture book art class at the Kansas City Art Institute with artist and teacher Wes Benson.

This book would not have been possible without my parents. For that reason, it is written for all parents/caregivers/educators who want to do the best for kids.

Knowledge is power, yet setting a personal example of moderation, exercise and good food choices is key. Most importantly, the individuality and uniqueness of every child must be respected to achieve positive and realistic health outcomes.

Rob Peters created the book illustrations. His amazing talent has made this story come alive.

I appreciate family, friends and colleagues who reviewed this manuscript.

Note To Parents/Caregivers/Educators

This personal story with a professional response was written to suggest, in picture book form, changes necessary to guide children to achieve a well-balanced diet and healthy lifestyle with support from their family.

The key concepts presented in this book are:

- Improving sensitivity to the needs of kids who are overweight;

- Suggesting children, no matter what shape or size, eat wholesome, healthy food and participate in daily physical activity;

- Increasing awareness of peer pressure, bullying and/or emotional vulnerabilities that may be experienced by a child who is overweight;

- Looking at factors that may contribute to a child's reluctance or inability to participate in a healthy lifestyle;

- Implementing school wellness policies that support physical activity, health and nutrition education with sensitivity to children of all shapes, sizes and abilities;

- Seeking professional weight management advice, counseling and/or coaching from a Registered Dietitian Nutritionist or other qualified health professional.

Dietary elements outlined in this story include:

- Evaluating all the components of the diet and eating pattern;

- Reviewing the foods that are brought into the home and food preparation methods;

- Substituting processed food with alternatives that are naturally low in fat, sugar and salt;

- Using portion control for meals and snacks;

- Selecting and eating "real" foods that represent the colors of the rainbow;

- Fitting a treat into the daily food plan;

- Sharing meals together;

- Teaching kids how to contribute to the preparation of meals and snacks.

Physical and recreational activity recommendations include the following for children:

- Participating in 60 minutes or more of daily physical activity;

- Encouraging the development of a wide variety of interests and activities to fill days with new and creative experiences.

Hello, I'm Roni.

Some kids think I am a boy because of my name. Most of the time I let it slide off my shoulder and ignore their teasing.

Sometimes kids joke about my appearance.
Now, **that hurts.**

My best friend Rosa rides with me on the
school bus. No matter what Rosa eats, she
looks the same. *It's just not fair!*

I live in an apartment building in the city with my parents and dog, Suki. There are many apartment buildings and stores in my neighborhood, with no playground in sight.

8

Our apartment is located on the 6th floor. Even though there are stairs in the building to walk up or down, Mom and I always **take the elevator.**

After school, Rosa comes over to play. I always have an afternoon **snack in front of the TV.**

My favorite snack is candy. I love to sit with a bowl of it on my lap that is filled with all the colors of the rainbow.

Since Dad comes home late from work,
Mom waits to have dinner with him.

We pick up **fast food** for me. I like the
fried chicken with mashed potatoes. I have
dinner early and **by myself.**

11

Today, I am a bit **scared.** The class is going to visit the school nurse's office. **This is not my most fun thing to do.**

What really **embarrasses me** is that everyone can see when the nurse weighs me. *NO CURTAINS!!!*

In gym class, we do all sorts of activities — push-ups, relays, jumping jacks and running — to test our physical health. **It's hard for me to keep up ...**

I hate to come in last all the time.

13

Mom didn't know what to do. She called a neighbor, Ms. Burnett, who is a **dietitian** for a local hospital. Mom told me a dietitian is a health professional with a college degree and training in foods and nutrition.

Ms. Burnett asked if she could come by and visit with us to get to know the family.

I didn't know what to expect!!!

Mom, Ms. Burnett and I sat at the kitchen table. Ms. Burnett asked me all sorts of questions, like —

What are my favorite foods and snacks?

What time do I eat, and who do I eat with?

Which types of activities do I like?

How often do I participate in sports or other physical activities?

And, more questions ...

I didn't know all the answers cause I NEVER REALLY THOUGHT ABOUT IT. Mom didn't either.

Ms. Burnett asked Mom for permission to go through our kitchen cabinets and refrigerator. She started taking things out and placing them on the counter top ...

Things like —

whole milk

sugar-sweetened
soda/pop

bags of chips

packaged cupcakes

fried chicken

white bread, bagels,
pasta and more

my favorite candy

Ms. Burnett said that some packaged and processed foods, are loaded with **fat, sugar and salt.**

She insisted that simple food changes would benefit the whole family.

skim or low-fat milk

water

baked chips

fresh fruit and vegetables

chicken without the skin

whole grain breads, cereals and pasta

Moderation is Key.

Ms. Burnett said to eat a reasonable amount of a variety of foods every day. Even candy can fit in.

Now, Mom prepares meals that reflect the rainbow.

1 cup of skim milk

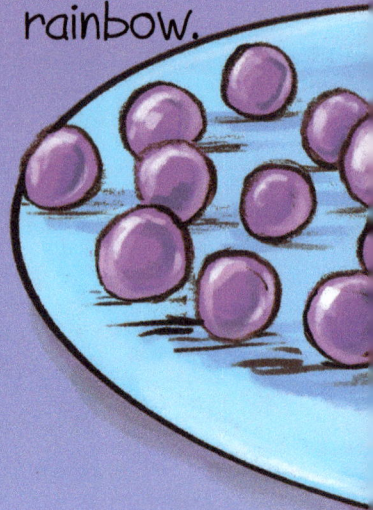

12 grapes for dessert

baked chicken leg, no skin

one-half ear of corn

½ cup carrots

½ cup fresh green beans

Beginning Monday morning, Mom passed the elevator and took me **down the stairs** in the apartment building, and then **up the stairs** after school.

Mom enrolled me in a **dance class** at the local Y two afternoons during the week. According to Ms. Barnett, I am supposed to get **60 minutes** or more of physical activity every day. WOW ...

Mom, Dad and I started eating dinner together most nights. Suki is never far from the table. Families that eat together make healthier food choices and can enjoy each other's company.

Mom even lets me help her in the kitchen. I enjoy making the salad. Yes, she lets me use a knife to cut up the veggies!!!

The hardest part of this healthy lifestyle plan is **limiting TV.** Instead of watching my favorite cartoons after school, I invite Rosa over to draw and color our favorite pictures with my new art kit.

Best of all, Mom reads a story to me every night.

Well, I guess it's all about **choices** and **balance** — eating the right foods, including daily physical activity, doing fun things and, of course, completing my homework.

I am on my way to a healthier and happier me. I **look better** in my jeans and **feel better,** too!!!

My new motto is, "Doing is freeing. Free to be the best that I can be."

Get to Know Yourself
for Better Health

Below are a series of questions that educators/parents/ caretakers can use to have a discussion with kids about their eating and lifestyle practices.

What is your favorite snack?

How often do you eat it?

Do you eat breakfast at home before school?

Is breakfast available at school?

Do you participate in the school lunch program?

If so, what do you like to get for lunch in the school cafeteria?

Do you prefer to bring your own lunch to school?

If so, what kinds of food are packed in your lunch box?

Whom do you eat dinner with at home?

What do you like to have for dinner?

Who is your closest friend?

What types of activities do you enjoy together?

Do you like to dance to your favorite song or recording group?

What fun games do you like to play?

Do you have a hobby or a special collection?

What television shows do you tune in to?

How long do you watch TV every day?

Do you like to play computer games? Which ones?

How much time do you spend in front of the computer every day?

Do you participate in sports? Which one(s)?

What other physical activities do you like?

Do you go to the local community center for exercise or to take dance classes?

Is there a place to play outside your home? What do you like to do when you play outside?

What is your favorite class in school?

Do you enjoy gym class? Which gym activities do you like best?

What is your most cherished object? A book? A special outfit? Bicycle? A birthday present?

If you could take a trip someplace, where would you go? What would you do there?

If you found out a friend or classmate was being treated badly, what would you do?

How can you show support for a classmate who may have a special need or disability or just look different?

If you had one wish that would change the world, what would it be?

Online U.S. Government Resources

Department of Agriculture (USDA)
Center for Nutrition Policy and Promotion
My Plate

http://www.choosemyplate.gov

Department of Health and Human Services (DHHS)
Centers for Disease Control and Prevention
Nutrition Topic Information

http://www.cdc.gov/nutrition

Information on Food and Nutrition for Consumers

http://www.nutrition.gov

National Institute of Child Health and Human
Development (NICHD)

http://www.nichd.nih.gov

National Institute on Minority Health and Health
Disparities (NIMHD)

http://www.nimhd.nih.gov

National Institutes of Health (NIH),
Office of Disease Prevention

http://prevention.nih.gov

About the Author

As an advanced-level nutrition practitioner, **Dr. Roni Roth Beshears** has worked at the local, state, and federal levels with food and nutrition programs and services. As a community volunteer and advocate, she has devoted time and energy to serving the needs of vulnerable women, children and families. Dr. Roth Beshears is a registered dietitian nutritionist and certified health and wellness coach. She is a graduate of Syracuse University (BS) and Columbia University, Teachers College (EdD).

www.ingramcontent.com/pod-product-compliance
Lightning Source LLC
Chambersburg PA
CBHW040257100426
42811CB00011B/1294